AUSSIE SLANG LING

AUSTRALIAN ENGLISH DICTIONARY

A

Acca Dacca
AC/DC.

Ace!
Excellent! very good.

Aerial Pingpong
Australian Rules Football.

After Dark
Rhyming slang for shark.

Aggro
Aggressive, ticked off, spoiling for a fight.

Akubra
A wide brimmed felt hat used for protection from sun.

Albany Doctor
Refreshing afternoon sea breeze in South West Australia.

Alf
A stupid person.

Alkie
An alcoholic.

All Froth And No Beer
A wasy to describe someone who is stupid.

All Piss And Wind
Full of shit.

All Wool And A Yard Wide
Authentic and trustworthy.

Alley Up
To pay back a debt.

Alligator
Horse.

Amber Fluid
Beer.

Ambo
An ambulance or ambulance driver.

Ankle Biter
A small child.

Any Tic Of The Clock
Very soon.

Apple Eater
Someone from Tasmania.

Apple Isle
Tasmania.

Arvo
Afternoon.

As Busy As A Cat Burying Shit
Busy.

As Cross As A Frog In A Sock
A person sounding angry.

As Dry As A Dead Dingo's Donger
Very dry.

As Dry As A Nun's Nasty
Dry.

As Dry As A Pommy's Towel
Very dry (based on a pom bathing once a month).

As Fit As A Mallee Bull
Very fit and strong.

As Full As A Goog
Drunk.

As Mean As Cat's Piss
Mean, stingy or uncharitable.

Aussie
Australian.

Aussie Battler
An ordinary Australian trying to make ends meet.

Aussie Salute
Brushing away flies with the hand.

Australian As Meat Pie
Typically or authentically Australian.

Australia's Little Brother
New Zealand.

Autumn Leaf
A jockey who continually falls off his horse.

Avos
Avocados.

B

B&S
Bachelors' and spinsters' ball - a party usually held in rural areas.

Baccy
Rolling tobacco.

Back Of Bourke
A very long way away.

Bag Of Fruit
Rhyming slang for suit.

Bail Out
Depart, usually angrily.

Bail Up
To corner somebody physically.

Banana Bender
A person from Queensland.

Bangers
Sausages.

Barbie
Barbecue.

Barney
An argument or fight.

Barra
Barramundi. A type of fish.

Barrack
To cheer on a football team etc.

Basso
Bassendean in Western Australia.

Bastard
A term of endearment.

Bathers
Swimming costume.

Bats
Crazy.

Battler
Someone working hard and only just making a living.

Baysie
Bayswater in Victoria.

Bazzaland
Australia.

Bean Counter
An accountant.

Beaut
Great, fantastic.

Beauty
Great, fantastic.

Bee's Dick
Smallest possible (eg chance of winning something).

Belly South
Belgrave South, Victoria.

Berk
An idiot or fool.

Bevo
Beverly Hills, New South Wales.

Beyond The Black Stump
A long way away, the back of nowhere.

Big Smoke
Big city or town.

Big-Note
To brag or boast.

Bikkie
A biscuit.

Billabong
A watering hole or pond in a dry riverbed.

Billy
A teapot or other container for boiling water.

Billy Lids
The kids.

Bingle
Motor vehicle accident.

Bities
Biting insects.

Bitzer
Mongrel dog.

Bizzo
Business, as in mind your own bizzo.

Bloke
A man, male guy.

Bloody
Very.

Bloody Oath!
That's certainly true.

Blow In The Bag
Have a breathalyser test.

Blowie
A blow fly.

Blow-In
A newcomer.

Bludger
A lazy person or somebody who always relies on other people to do things for them.

Blue
A fight.

Bluey
Blue cattle dog (a working dog).

Bluey
Heavy wool or felt jacket worn by mining and construction workers.

Bluey
Bluebottle jellyfish.

Bodgy
Of inferior quality.

Bog In
To commence eating with enthusiasm.

Bog Standard
Basic.

Bogan
Person who takes little pride in his appearance and who spends his days being lazy & drinking beer. An Aussie redneck.

Bogged
A vehicle stuck in deep sand or mud.

Bondi Cigar
A turd in the sea (also brown-eyed mullet).

Bonzer
Great.

Boogie Board
A hybrid, half-sized surf board.

Boomer
A large kangaroo.

Booze Bus
Police vehicle used for catching drunk drivers.

Boozer
A pub.

Bored Shitless
Very bored.

Bottle Shop
A liquor shop.

Bottle-O
A liquor shop.

Bottler
Something excellent.

Bounce
A bully.

Bouncy Mouse
Kangaroo.

Bread Basket
Your stomach.

Brekkie
Breakfast.

Brickie
Bricklayer.

Bring A Plate
Instruction on a party or barbecue invitation to bring your own food.

Brisangeles
Brisbane, Queensland.

Brisneyland
Brisbane, the state capital of Queensland.

Brisvegas
Brisbane, Queensland.

Brizzie
Brisbane, the state capital of Queensland.

Brown-Eyed Mullet
A turd in the sea (also bondi cigar).

Brumby
A wild horse.

Buck
One dollar - $1.

Buck's Night
A stag party. A male gathering the night before the wedding.

Buckley's Chance
No chance.

Budgie Smugglers
Men's speedos.

Bugalugs
A friendly term of endearment.

Built Like A Brick Shit House
Big strong bloke.

Bull Bar
A bar fixed to the front of a vehicle to protect it against hitting kangaroos (also roo bar).

Bull Dust
A lie.

Bun In The Oven
Pregnant.

Bunch Of Fives
A punch or fist.

Bundy
Short for Bundaberg, Queensland, and the brand of rum that's made there.

Bunyip
Mythical outback creature.

Bush
The outback or anywhere that isn't in town.

Bush Bash
Long competitive running or car race through the bush.

Bush Oyster
Nasal mucus.

Bush Telly
Campfire.

Bushie
Someone who lives in the bush.

Bushman'S Clock
A kookaburra.

Bushman'S Hanky
Emitting nasal mucus by placing a finger on the outside of the nose to one nostril and blowing.

Bushranger
Highwayman.

Bushwalking
Hiking or walking in the bush for pleasure.

Bushweek
An exclamation that you don't believe what they are telling you.

Bust A Gut
Work hard or to put in effort.

Buster
Strong wind.

Butcher
Small glass of beer in South Australia.

Byo
A restaurant, party or barbecue where you have to bring your own alcohol.

C

Cab Sav
Cabernet Sauvignon (a variety of wine grape).

Cabbage Patcher
Resident of Victoria.

Cabbie
Taxi driver.

Cackleberry
An egg.

Cactus
Dead, no longer functioning.

Cake Hole
Mouth.

Cane Toad
A person from Queensland.

Captain Cook
Rhyming slang for have a look.

Carbie
A vehicle carburetor.

Cark It
To die or stop functioning.

Carpet Grub
Small child.

Cattle Duffer
Stupid or incompetent person.

Cattle Duffer
A cattle thief.

Centralia
The inland region of Australia.

Chalkie
A teacher.

Cheerio
Goodbye.

Chew And Spew
A cheap cafe.

Chewie
Chewing gum.

Chips
French-fries.

Choc-A-Block
Completely full.

Chokkie
Chocolate.

Chook
A chicken.

Choom
Englishman.

Choppers
Teeth.

Chrissie
Christmas.

Chubbers
Shoes.

Chuck A Sickie
Take the day off sick from work when you're feeling perfectly fine and healthy to go in.

Chunder
Vomit.

Clacker
Anus.

Clacker
The single orifice of a monotreme (platypus and echidna) used both for reproduction and for the elimination of body waste.

Clayton's
Fake.

Cleanskin
Bottle of wine without a label. Usually bought in bulk by companies who then add their own label for use as gifts to clients.

Cleanskin
Cattle that have not been branded, earmarked or castrated.

Click
One kilometre.

Clod Hoppers
Feet.

Clucky
Feeling broody or maternal.

Coat Hanger
Sydney Harbour Bridge.

Cobber
A good friend.

Cockie
Farmer.

Cockie
Cockatoo.

Cockie
Cockroach.

Cockroach
A person from New South Wales.

Coldie
A beer.

Come A Gutser
Make a bad mistake or have an accident.

Come Off The Grass
Do you think i'm stupid?

Come The Raw Prawn
To lie or to be generally disagreeable.

Compo
Workers' compensation pay.

Conch
A conscientious person who would rather work or study than go out and enjoy themselves.

Cook
Someone's wife.

Copper
Policeman.

Corker
Something excellent.

Corroboree
An Aboriginal dance festival.

Counter Lunch
Pub lunch.

Countery
Pub lunch.

Cow Juice
Milk from a cow.

Cozzie
A swimming costume.

Crack A Fat
To get an erection.

Crack Onto (Someone)
To hit on someone or pursue them romantically.

Cranky
In a bad mood, angry.

Cranny
Cranbourne, Victoria.

Cream
Defeat by a large margin.

Crikey
Blimey or holy sh*t.

Crikey Mikey
A Snake.

Croc
A crocodile.

Crook
Sick or badly made.

Crow Eater
A person from South Australia.

Cruisy
Easy.

Cubby House
Small timber house in the garden used as a children's plaything.

Cunning As A Dunny Rat
Very cunning.

Cuppa
Cup of tea.

Cut Lunch
Sandwiches.

Cut Lunch Commando
Army reservist.

D

Dag
A nerd, funny person or goof.

Daggy
Something that looks untidy or bad.

Daks
Trousers.

Damper
Bread made from flour and water.

Dangarang
Awesome.

Date
Arse.

Date Roll
Roll of toilet paper.

Dead Horse
Rhyming slang for sauce.

Dead Horse
Tomato sauce.

Dead Marine
Empty beer bottle.

Dead Ringer
An exact copy or likeness.

Dead-Cert
Definite or certain.

Deadset
True.

Dero
A homeless person, tramp.

Dial
Face.

Dickhead
An idiot. Somebody who talks drivel with whom you have little patience.

Didgeri-Don't
Stop.

Didgeridoo
Aboriginal musical instrument.

Digger
An Australian soldier.

Dill
An idiot.

Dingaling
A silly person.

Dingbat
A fool or immature person.

Dingo
An Australian wild dog.

Dingo's Breakfast
No breakfast.

Dinkum, Fair Dinkum
True, real, genuine.

Dinky-Di
The real thing, genuine.

Dip
Swim.

Dipstick
A loser, idiot.

Divvy Van
Police vehicle used for transporting criminals.

Dob In
Inform on somebody.

Dobber
A tell-tale.

Docket
A bill or receipt.

Doco
A documentary.

Dog
An unattractive woman.

Dog's Eye
Meat pie.

Dogereedoo
A puppy.

Dole Bludger
Somebody on social assistance when unjustified.

Donger
Penis.

Donk
A car or boat engine.

Doodah
A think woth a name that is forgotten.

Doodle
Penis.

Dork
A person with little personality.

Down The John
Off to the toilet.

Down Under
Australia and New Zealand.

Drink With The Flies
To drink alone.

Drongo
A stupid person.

Dropkick
A loser, idiot.

Dropped Your Guts
You have farted.

Drum
Information or tip-off.

Duchess
Sideboard.

Dudder
An unscrupulous person that cheats others.

Duds
Trousers.

Dunny
Outside lavatory.

Dunny Budgie
Blowfly.

Durry
Tobacco, cigarette.

Dust Eaters
People who live in the Northern Territory.

Dux
Top of the class.

E

Earbashing
Nagging, non-stop chatter.

Easterner
A Western Australian term for a person from the Eastern States.

Easy As Pushing Shit Uphill With A Toothpick
Extremely difficult.

Eating With The Flies
Eating alone.

Egg Beater
A helicopter.

Egg On
Encourage or persuade a hesitant person.

Ekka
The Brisbane exhibition, an annual show.

Elephant's Trunk
Rhyming slang for drunk.

En Zed
New Zealand.

Esky
Large insulated food or drink container for picnics, barbecues etc.

Exercise Book
School workbook.

Exy
Expensive.

F

Face Fungus
Beard.

Fag
Cigarette.

Fair Dinkum
True, real, genuine.

Fair Go
A chance.

Fair Go Mate
Give me a chance.

Fair Suck Of The Sav
Exclamation of wonder, awe or disbelief.

Fairy Floss
Candy floss.

Fang Carpenter
Dentist.

Fang It
Drive fast.

Farmer Giles
Rhyming slang for piles or haemorrhoids.

Feral
A hippie.

Feral
A V8 ute with a large heavy bullbar, aerials, large mudflaps and stickers all over the rear window and tailgate.

Figjam
Nickname for people who have a high opinion of themselves.

Finnegan's Hole
Car trunk.

Fisho
Fishmonger.

Flake
Shark's flesh sold in fish & chips shops.

Flat Out Like A Lizard Drinking
Busy.

Flat White
Coffee with milk.

Flick
To get rid of somthing or someone.

Flick It On
To sell something, usually for a quick profit, soon after buying it.

Floater
Meat pie in a bowl of peas or gravy (South Australian).

Fly Wire
Gauze flyscreen covering a window or doorway.

Footy
Australian Rules Football.

Fossick
Search, rummage.

Franger
Condom.

Freckle
Anus.

Fremantle Doctor
The cooling afternoon breeze that arrives in perth from the direction of Freo.

Freo
Fremantle in Western Australia.

Freshie
Tourist.

Fruit Loop
Fool.

Full
Drunk.

Funny As A Fart In An Elevator
Not funny.

Furphy
False or unreliable rumour.

G

G'day
Hello.

Gabba
Wooloongabba - the Brisbane cricket ground.

Gafa
The big nothingness of the Australian outback.

Galah
A noisy foolish person.

Gander
To have a look at.

Garbo
Garbage collector.

Garbologist
Garbage collector.

Garlic Muncher
Someone from Central or Southern Europe.

Gasbag
A person who talks a lot.

Get The Pink Slip
Get the sack. It is the colour of the termination form.

Get Up Somebody
To rebuke somebody.

Ginger Meggs
Rhyming slang for legs.

Give A Gobful
To abuse verbally.

Give It A Burl
Try it, have a go.

Gobsmacked
Surprised, astounded.

Going Off
Used of a night spot or party that is a lot of fun.

Gone Troppo
Gone crazy.

Good Nick
In good condition.

Good Oil
Useful information, a good idea, the truth.

Good Onya
Good for you, well done.

Goose
Someone who is not smart and does silly things.

Got The Wobbly Boot On
Drunk.

Greenie
An environmentalist.

Gregory Peck
Neck.

Grinning Like A Shot Fox
Very happy, smugly satisfied.

Grog
liquor, beer.

Grot
To be dirty or untidy.

Grouse
Great, terrific, very good.

Grundies
Undies, underwear.

Gumsucker
Someone who lives in the state of Victoria.

Gurgler
Plughole that goes down a drain into the sewer.

Gutful Of Piss
Drunk.

Gyno
Gynaecologist.

H

Half Your Luck
Congratulations or best wishes.

Handle
Beer glass with a handle.

Hard Yakka
Hard work.

Have A Lend Of
To have someone on or to take advantage of somebody's gullibility.

Have A Naughty
Have sex.

He Doesn't Know Christmas From Bourke Street
He's a bit slow in the head. Bourke Street is a brightly lit Melbourne street.

He Hasn't Got A Brass Razoo
He's very poor.

Heaps
A lot.

Heave
To be sick.

His Blood's Worth Bottling
He's an excellent, helpful bloke.

His Nibs
The boss or head of a group.

Holy Dooley!
An exclamation of surprise.

Hoof It
To walk rather than take transport.

Hoon
Hooligan.

Hooroo
Goodbye.

Hotel
Often just a pub.

Hottie
Hot water bottle.

I

I Feel Stuffed
I'm tired.

I'll Be Stuffed
Expression of surprise.

Ice Block
Popsicle, lollypop.

Icy Pole
Popsicle, lollypop.

Idiot Box
Television.

In The Altogether
Naked.

In The Nuddy
Naked.

Ipshit
Ipswich, Queensland.

It Cost Big Bikkies
It was expensive.

It's Gone Walkabout
It's lost, can't be found.

Ivories
Your teeth.

J

Jackaroo
A male trainee station manager or station hand.

Jiffy
Short period of time.

Jillaroo
A female trainee station manager or station hand.

Joe Bloggs
Average person on the street.

Joey
Baby kangaroo.

Journo
Journalist.

Jug
Electric kettle.

Jumbuck
Sheep.

K

Kangaroos Loose In The Top Paddock
Intellectually inadequate.

Kark It
To die.

Kelpie
Australian sheepdog originally bred from Scottish Collie.

Kero
Kerosene.

Kindie
Kindergarten.

Kip
A short nap.

Kiwi
A person from New Zealand.

Knock
To criticise.

Knock Back
To refuse.

Knocker
Somebody who criticises.

Koala Log
Cigarette.

L

Lair
A flashily dressed young man of brash and vulgar behaviour.

Lair
To renovate or dress up something in bad taste.

Lair It Up
To behave in a brash and vulgar manner.

Lamington
Sponge cake cut into squares and covered in chocolate and coconut.

Larrikin
A bloke who is always enjoying himself, a harmless prankster.

Lay By
To buy something on credit and pay it off in installments over a period of time.

Lead Foot
Someone who drives fast.

Lino
Linoleum.

Lippy
Lipstick.

Liquid Laugh
Vomit.

Livo
Ipswich, Queensland.

Lob In
Drop in to see someone.

Local Rag
The local newspaper.

Lollies
Sweets, candy.

Lolly
Money.

London To A Brick
Absolute certainty.

Long Paddock
The side of the road where livestock is grazed during droughts.

Longneck
750ml bottle of beer in South Australia.

Loo
Toilet.

Lubra
Adult female Aboriginal.

Lurk
Illegal or underhanded racket.

M

Maccas
The fast good chain, Mcdonald's.

Mad As A Cut Snake
Very angry.

Make A Blue
Make a mistake.

Make A Quid
Earn a living.

Manchester
Household linen.

Mappa Tassie
The female pubic region. Similarity in shape with the roughly triangular form of Tasmania.

Mate
Buddy, friend.

Mate's Discount
Cheaper than usual for a friend.

Mate's Rate
Cheaper than usual for a friend.

Matilda
Swagman's bedding, sleeping bag.

Metho
Methylated spirits.

Mexican
A person from South of the Queensland or New South Wales border.

Mickey Mouse
In some parts of Australia it means frivolous or not very good.

Mickey Mouse
Excellent, very good.

Middy
285 ml beer glass in New South Wales.

Milk Bar
Corner shop that sells takeaway food.

Milko
Milkman.

Mob
Group of people, not necessarily troublesome.

Mob
Family or group of kangaroos.

Mollycoddle
Fuss over or baby someone.

Mongrel
Despicable person.

Moolah
Money.

Mother Union
The moon.

Mozzie
Mosquito.

Mucking Around
Playing around with no purpose.

Muddy
Mud crab (a delicacy).

Mug
Friendly insult, gullible person.

Mulga
The outback.

Mull
Grass of the kind you smoke.

Muster
Round up sheep or cattle.

Mystery Bag
A sausage.

N

Nasho
National service.

Never Never
The outback, centre of Australia.

Nick
To steal.

Nipper
Young surf lifesaver.

No Drama
No worries.

No Worries!
No problem, forget about it.

Noggin
Head.

No-Hoper
Somebody who'll never do well.

Nong
Idiot.

Not My Bowl Of Rice
Not my cup of tea or i don't like it.

Not The Full Quid
Of low IQ.

Not Within Cooee
A long way away or far off.

Nut Out
Work out something.

O

O.S.
Overseas.

Ocker
An unsophisticated person.

Off One'S Face
Drunk.

Offsider
An assistant, helper.

Old Cheese
Mother.

Old Fella
Penis.

Old Man
Father or husband.

Old Woman
Mother or wife.

Oldies
Parents.

On For Young And Old
A fight or argument involving everyone.

On The Nose
Smells terrible, stinky.

Op Shop
Opportunity shop. a place where second hand goods are sold.

Open Slather
Anything goes.

Outback
The interior of Australia.

Oz
Australia.

Ozzies
Australians.

P

Pack A Wallop
Punch someone hard.

Paddock
The side of the road where livestock is grazed during droughts.

Palmy
Palm Beach, New South Wales.

Panel Beater
Car repair shop or person.

Pash
A long passionate kiss.

Pav
Pavlova.

Perve
Looking lustfully at the opposite sex.

Pictures
Movie theatre, cinema.

Piece Of Piss
Easy task.

Pig's Arse
I don't agree with you.

Piker
Someone who doesn't want to fit in with others socially, leaves parties early.

Pint
Large glass of beer.

Piss
Beer.

Plodder
Slow and steady worker.

Plonk
Cheap wine.

Pokies
Poker, fruit, gambling or slot machines.

Polly
Politician.

Pom
An Englishman.

Pommy
An Englishman.

Pommy Bastard
An Englishman.

Pommy Shower
Using deodorant instead of taking a shower.

Porky
Lie.

Port
Suitcase (portmanteau).

Postie
Postman, mailman.

Pot
285 ml beer glass in Queensland and Victoria.

Pozzy
Position.

Pretty Spiffy
Great, excellent.

Prezzy
Present, gift.

Puffed
Out of breath.

Push Bike
Bicycle.

Push Off
Get lost! get out of here.

R

Rack Off
Get lost! get out of here.

Rack Off Hairy Legs
Get lost! get out of here.

Rag
Local newspaper.

Rage
Party.

Rage On
To continue partying.

Rapt
Pleased, delighted.

Ratbag
Mild insult.

Reckon
You bet! Absolutely.

Reffo
Refugee.

Rego
Vehicle registration.

Rellie
Family relative.

Relo
Family relative.

Ridgy-Didge
Original, genuine.

Rip Snorter
Great, fantastic.

Ripper
Great, fantastic.

Road Train
Big truck with many trailers.

Rock Up
To arrive.

Rollie
A cigarette that you roll yourself.

Ron
See you later.

Roo
Kangaroo.

Roo Bar
Stout bar fixed to the front of a vehicle to protect it against hitting kangaroos (also bull bar).

Root
Synonym for f*ck in nearly all its senses. Mainly used in polite company.

Root Rat
Somebody who is constantly looking for sex.

Ropeable
Very angry.

Rort
Cheating, fiddling, defrauding. It is usually used of politicians.

Rotten
Drunk.

Rubbish
To criticise.

S

Sack
Bed.

Saffa
South African.

Salvos
Salvation Army.

Sambo
Sandwich.

Sand Shoes
Canvas sneakers.

Sandgroper
A person from Western Australia.

Sanger
A sandwich.

Sav
Saveloy.

Schooner
Large beer glass in Queensland, medium beer glass in South Australia.

Scratchy
Instant lottery ticket.

Screamer
Party lover.

Scrub
The bush but with fewer and shorter trees.

Scubbers
Cattle in the wild.

Seppo
An American.

Septic Tank
Yank. Rhyming slang for an American.

Servo
Petrol station.

Shaky Isles
New Zealand.

Shark Biscuit
Somebody new to surfing.

She Right
It'll be all right.

She'll Be Apples
It'll be all right.

She'll Be Right
It'll turn out okay.

Sheepshagger
A New Zealander.

Sheila
A woman.

Shit House
Of poor quality, unenjoyable.

Shit House
Toilet, lavatory.

Shonky
Dubious, underhanded.

Shoot Through
To leave.

Shout
Usually a turn to buy a round of drinks.

Show Pony
Someone who tries hard by his dress or behaviour, usually to impress those around him.

Sickie
Day off sick from work.

Sin City
Sydney, New South Wales.

Skint
Out of money, broke.

Skippy
An Australian or kangaroo.

Skite
Boast, brag.

Skull
To drink a beer in a single draught without taking a breath.

Slab
A carton of 24 bottles or cans of beer.

Sleepout
House verandah converted to a bedroom.

Sleeve Urwins
Sweatshirt.

Slumshine
Sunshine, Victoria.

Smoko
Smoke or coffee break.

Snag
A sausage.

Snow Job
A con job.

Sook
Person who is sulking.

Spag Bol
Spaghetti bolognese.

Spewin'
Very angry.

Spiffy
Great, excellent.

Spit The Dummy
Get very upset at something.

Spot On
Perfect, exactly.

Spruiker
Man who stands outside a nightclub or restaurant trying to persuade people to enter.

Sprung
Caught doing something wrong.

Spunk
A good looking person of either sex.

Squizz
To look at something.

Standover Man
A large man, usually gang-related, who threatens people with physical violence to have his wishes carried out.

Stands Out Like A Shag On A Rock
Very obvious.

Stands Out Like Dog's Balls
Obvious.

Station
A big farm or grazing property.

Sticky-Beak
Nosey person.

Stoked
Very pleased.

Stonkered
Drunk.

Storm-Stick
Umbrella.

Straya
Australia.

Strewth
Exclamation, mild oath.

Strides
Trousers.

Strine
Australian slang and pronunciation.

Struth
An exclamation expressing surprise.

Stubby
A 375ml beer bottle.

Stubby Holder
Polystyrene insulated holder for a stubby.

Stunned Mullet
Clueless, surprised or stunned facial expression.

Sunbake
Sunbathe.

Sunnies
Sunglasses.

Surfies
People who go surfing.

Swag
Rolled up bedding etc. carried by a swagman.

Swaggie
Swagman.

Swagman
Tramp, hobo.

T

Ta
Thank you.

Take Away
A take out.

Talking On The Porcelain Telephone
Vomiting into a toilet.

Tall Poppies
Successful people.

Tall Poppy Syndrome
The tendency to criticise successful people.

Tallie
750ml bottle of beer.

Taswegian
Derogatory term for a person from Tasmania.

Taxi Rank
Taxi stand.

Technicolor Yawn
Vomit.

Tee-Up
To set up something like an appointment.

Ten Ounce Sandwich
Lunch consisting of only beer.

That'D Be Right
Accepting bad news as inevitable.

The Alice
Alice Springs, a town in the Northern territory of Australia.

The Berra
Canberra

The Lucky Country
Australia.

The Singing Budgie
Kylie Minogue.

Thingo
That thing, what do you call it? A term used for something you can't remeber the name of.

Thongs
Cheap rubber backless sandals.

Throw-Down
Small bottle of beer which you can throw down quickly.

Ticker
The heart.

Tin-Arsed Tinny
Lucky.

Tinny
Can of beer.

Tinny
Small aluminium boat.

To Come The Raw Prawn
To be disagreeable or to bullshit.

To Do The Harold
To bolt.

To Do The Harold Holt
To bolt.

To Have On Oneself Tickets
To have a high opinion of oneself.

Togs
Swim suit.

Too Right
Definitely.

Top End
Far North of Australia.

Top Ender
A person from the Northern Territory.

Trackie Daks/Dacks
Tracksuit pants.

Trackies
A tracksuit.

Tradie
A tradesperson.

Trough Lolly
The solid piece of perfumed disinfectant that is found in a men's urinal.

Truckie
Truck driver.

True Blue
Patriotic or loyal friends and families.

Tucker
Food.

Tucker-Bag
Food bag.

Turps
Turpentine.

Turps
Alcoholic drink.

Turps, Hit The
Go on a drinking binge.

Two Pot Screamer
Somebody who gets drunk on very little alcohol.

Two Up
Gambling game played by spinning two coins simultaneously.

Tyke
A 3 to 6 year old small child.

U

U-Ee
A U turn in a vehicle.

Underground Mutton
A rabbit.

Uni
University.

Unit
Flat, apartment.

Up A Gum Tree
In a difficult situation or stranded.

Up Oneself
Have a high opinion of oneself.

Useful As An Ashtray On A Motorbike
Unhelpful or incompetent person or thing.

Useful As Tits On A Bull
Unhelpful or incompetent person or thing.

Ute
Utility vehicle, pickup truck.

V

VB
Victoria bitter, beer.

Vedgies
Vegetables.

Vee Dub
Volkswagen.

Veg Out
Relax in front of the tv.

Vejjo
Vegetarian.

Vics
People from Victoria.

Vinnie's
St. Vincent De Paul's (charity thrift stores and hostels).

Volcanoes
Pimples or boils.

W

Waca
Western Australian Cricket Association and the Perth cricket ground.

Waggin' School
Playing truant.

Walkabout
A hike.

Walkabout
Lost or not found.

Wally Grout
Rhyming slang for shout.

Waltzing Matilda
Wander aimlessly through the bush.

Water The Horse
To urinate.

Weekend Warrior
Army reservist.

West Auckland
Bondi, New South Wales.

Westie
Someone from the Western suburbs of Sydney.

Whacka
An idiot. Somebody who talks nonesense. A dickhead.

Whacker
Somebody who talks drivel, an idiot. Somebody with whom you have little patience. Dickhead.

Wharfie
Dock worker.

Whinge
To complain.

White Pointers
Topless female sunbathers.

Whiteant
To criticise something to deter somebody from buying it.

Who Cut The Dog In Half?
Someone has farted.

Who Opened Their Lunch?
Ok, who farted?

Willy-Willy
A mini tornado.

Within Cooee
Nearby.

Wobbly
To become agitated or angry suddenly.

Wog
Flu or trivial illness.

Wombat
Somebody who eats, roots and leaves.

Woop Woop
Middle of nowhere.

Wowser
A prude person, spoilsport.

Wuss
Nervous person or animal or a coward.

X

XXXX
Brand of beer made in Queensland. It is pronounced four x.

Y

Yabber
Talk a lot.

Yabby
Inland freshwater crayfish found in Australia.

Yack
Get together to talk.

Yakka
Work.

Yank
An American.

Yarn
A long story.

Yeah Nah
No.

Yewy
A U-turn.

Yobbo
A person lacking good manners.

Yonks
A long period of time.

Yonnie
A flat stone or pebble suitable for skimming across water.

You Little Ripper
Exclamation of delight or as a reaction to good news.

Your Shout
Your turn to buy beer.

Yowie
A mythical Australian monster.

Z

Zack
Sixpence (5 cents).

Zebra Crossing
A black and white striped pedestrian crossing.

Ziff
Beard.

Printed in Great Britain
by Amazon